Life Journal

LIFE JOURNAL

A VISION BOARD THAT GOES WITH YOU!

CHRISTINE CORDERO

~

This book is dedicated to my daughters,
Angelica and Esmeralda.
Girls you are a blessing sent from God.

Contents

ACKNOWLEDGEMENTS

Contents

Acknowledgements

I want to thank a few special people who have provided me with love, guidance and inspiration in many ways:

Alana Byrne, deny as you may – you are my mother. I thank you for picking up the pieces when it was most needed.

Hewa (Ruth) Halverson, my mentor – your encouragement and support through my teenage years and beyond has given me with a greater understanding of the performing arts and your gentle influence has provided me with a compass on my mission to help others.

Lily Driscoll, you know I had to mention you. Thanks for being a true friend and welcoming my family into yours.

Beatitudes Community -
Debbie O., Tracey J., Elsa T., John & Kendra H., Carol T., Mary R., & Debbie V. (We miss ya!) – I couldn't ask for a better group to be in fellowship with.

Carmen Rodriguez and Laura Gonzalez; Ladies you both have been a wild ride of friendship since the first day we met. Thanks for being so supportive and full of energy.

Introduction

Welcome!

I prepared this book for you.

When I found out about LOA (Law of Attraction/ Abundance) you might say that it took my world by storm. I was so jazzed about viewing and living my life positively and I began to see changes happen so quickly. During the beginning phase I began looking for the 'tools' to get me to the next level. I searched for a journal to apply everything I was learning and did not find what I was looking for.

That was when I began to combining thoughts that were helpful, and I tweaked them into my own life journal. So when I was out on the beach, or on a train, or in the back seat on a road trip I could quickly write down a passing thought or a treasured experience. Most importantly, I began writing down what I wanted in my life, and carrying around a life journal similar to this one helped me to affirm my new approach to life.

I am so excited for you! My desire is that you begin your path to creating abundance in your life by writing your desires.

Remain positive, and keep notes wherever you are.
This journal is yours – write/draw in the margins. Have Fun!

Remain Blessed,
Christine

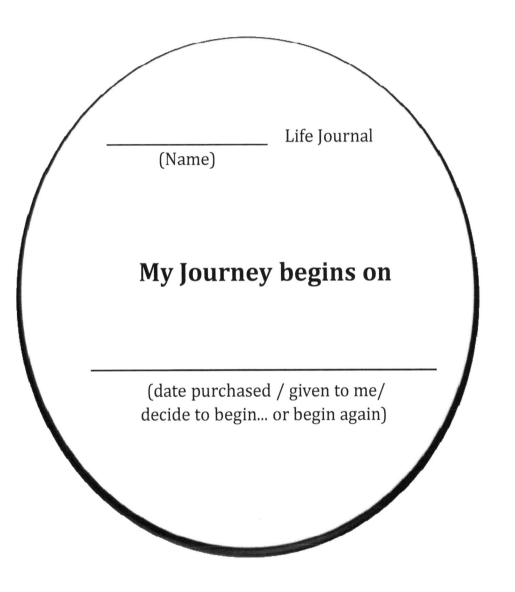

_____ Life Journal
        (Name)

My Journey begins on

_____

(date purchased / given to me/
decide to begin... or begin again)

Blending of the Minds

Positive Thinking

It is an attitude that expects good and promising results.

LOA

The Law of Attraction - draw into your life whatever you truly desire and your thoughts will find a way to manifest.

Affirmations

Expressions to implement positive changes in a persons life.

The Secret Stuff

Have FUN! Learn a new joke and tell it. Go beyond your personal boundaries, and try new things. See a funny movie. Take in the fresh air – Enjoy Life!

Overview

Envision yourself in a place where you have a continuous supply of all that you need to develop, maintain, or improve your life.

Luckily you don't have to go far...
because everything you need is within YOU!

Become your own dictionary
My Definition:– personalize
what each section means to you!

Take time to scribble!
Draw a scenario that you
would like to experience.

The Power of Words.
Use words that can help
describe what you would
like to attain.

art with great happiness?

eatest strengths?

How can I combine my happiness with my strengths?

Place YOUR ideas and desires on paper – get it out of your mind's eye. Search for your true desire.

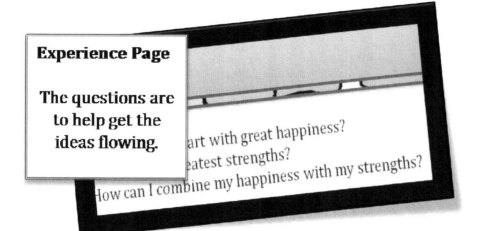

Affirmation Example

True Desire	Beginning Date	Ending Date	Outcome
			Completion
True Desire put into motion has only one option		UNKNOWN	FAMILY REUNION 7/08
DAUGHTERS MEET EXTENDED FAMILY	SUMMER 2004	UNKNOWN	2/06 – MET LAY! – BFF :)
HAVE A BEST FRIEND AGAIN	11/2005	UNKNOWN	FALL OF 2008
DAUGHTERS IN PRIVATE SCHOOL	1/2006	DEADLINE 12/2008	8/1208 – WOOHOO EARLIER! SOON!
LEAVE STRESSFUL JOB	2/2008	WITHIN THE YEAR	
PUBLISH LIFE JOURNAL BOOK	2/2008		

Visual Support

Inner Self

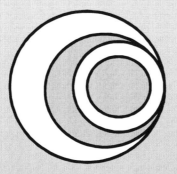

o Inner Self

o Future Self

o Individuality

o Self Awareness

o Ability

o Character

Envision Inner Self

My Definition:

Scribble

Inner Self Experience

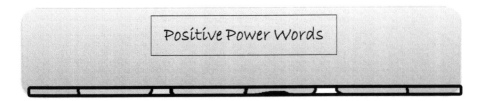

Positive Power Words

What fills my heart with great happiness?
What are my greatest strengths?
How can I combine my happiness with my strengths?

Inner Self

Visual
Support

Inner Self Affirmation

True Desire	Beginning Date	Ending Date	Outcome
True Desire put into motion has only one option ⟹			<u>Completion</u>
———	———	———	———
———	———	———	———
———	———	———	———
———	———	———	———
———	———	———	———
———	———	———	———
———	———	———	———
———	———	———	———
———	———	———	———

Inners Self Gratitude

Envision Future Self

My Definition:

Scribble

Future Self Experience

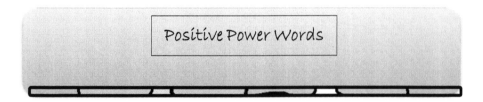

Positive Power Words

What are the qualities that I would like to improve or gain?
Who is the person that I want to be?
How do I want to be remembered?

Future Self

Visual
Support

Future Self Affirmation

True Desire	Beginning Date	Ending Date	Outcome
True Desire put into motion has only one option		→	Completion

Future Self Gratitude

Envision Individuality

My Definition:

Scribble

Individuality Experience

Positive Power Words

What makes me different / special from everyone else?
What are the good things that are in my life because of my
unique qualities?
How can I use these qualities more in the future?

Individuality

Visual
Support

Individuality Affirmation

True Desire	Beginning Date	Ending Date	Outcome
True Desire put into motion has only one option ➡			Completion

Individuality Gratitude

Envision Self Awareness

My Definition:

Scribble

Self Awareness Experience

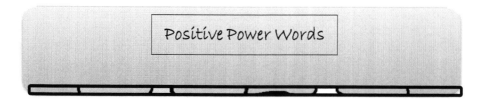

Positive Power Words

What are the common themes that keep reoccurring in my life?
How can I expand and grow within these themes?
How do these themes prepare me for my future?

Self Awareness

Visual
Support

Self Awareness Affirmation

True Desire	Beginning Date	Ending Date	Outcome
True Desire put into motion has only one option			Completion

Self Awareness Gratitude

Envision Ability

My Definition:

Scribble

Ability Experience

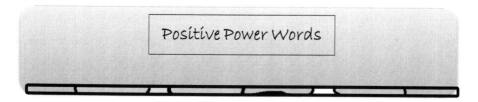

Positive Power Words

What are my top ten abilities?
Where do I apply these abilities in my life?
How do I want to expand on my abilities?

Ability

Visual
Support

Ability Affirmation

True Desire	Beginning Date	Ending Date	Outcome
True Desire put into motion has only one option ➡			<u>Completion</u>

Ability Gratitude

Envision Character

My Definition:

Scribble

Character Experience

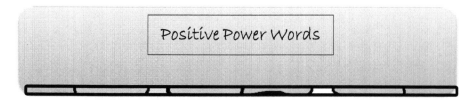

Positive Power Words

What are my positive character traits?
How do these traits help me in life?
Where do I apply my positive character strengths in my life?

Character

Visual
Support

Character Affirmation

True Desire	Beginning Date	Ending Date	Outcome
True Desire put into motion has only one option ➡			Completion
————	————	————	————
————	————	————	————
————	————	————	————
————	————	————	————
————	————	————	————
————	————	————	————
————	————	————	————
————	————	————	————
————	————	————	————
————	————	————	————

Character Gratitude

Connection

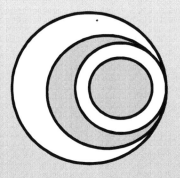

- ○ Connection
- ○ Spirituality
- ○ Relationships
- ○ Family Children
- ○ Community

Envision Connection

My Definition:

Scribble

Connection Experience

Positive Power Words

How do I connect with the world?
Where are my connections the strongest?
What connections do I want to create?

Connection

Visual
Support

Connection Affirmation

True Desire	Beginning Date	Ending Date	Outcome
**True Desire** put into motion has only one option ➡			<u>Completion</u>

Connection Gratitude

Envision Spirituality

My Definition:

Scribble

Spirituality Experience

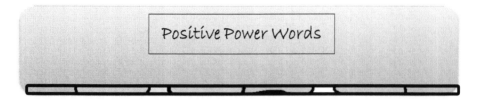

Positive Power Words

What is spirituality to me?
How does my spirituality help me in life?
What steps can I take to integrate spirituality my life?

Spirituality

Visual
Support

Spirituality Affirmation

True Desire	Beginning Date	Ending Date	Outcome
True Desire put into motion has only one option	→		Completion

Spirituality Gratitude

.

Envision Relationships

My Definition:

Scribble

Relationships Experience

Positive Power Words

What relationships are key to me in my life?
How can I encourage more positive relationships in my life?
What relationships would I like to strengthen / have?

Relationships

Visual
Support

Relationships Affirmation

True Desire	Beginning Date	Ending Date	Outcome
True Desire put into motion has only one option ➡			<u>Completion</u>

Relationships Gratitude

Envision Family

My Definition:

Scribble

Family Experience

What does family mean to me?
What is my greatest hope for my family?
In what ways can I strengthen my family?

Family

Visual
Support

Family Affirmation

True Desire	Beginning Date	Ending Date	Outcome
True Desire put into motion has only one option ➡			<u>Completion</u>

Family Gratitude

Envision Children

My Definition:

Scribble

Children Experience

Who are the children in my life?
What is my desire for these children?
How can I improve the life of a child/ children?

Children

Visual
Support

Children Affirmation

True Desire	Beginning Date	Ending Date	Outcome
True Desire put into motion has only one option ➡			Completion

Children Gratitude

Envision Community

My Definition:

Scribble

Community Experience

Positive Power Words

Where are my communities?
What role do I take in my communities?
What communities do I reconnect /interact with in the future?

Community

Visual
Support

Community Affirmation

True Desire	Beginning Date	Ending Date	Outcome
True Desire put into motion has only one option ➡			<u>Completion</u>

───	───	───	───
───	───	───	───
───	───	───	───
───	───	───	───
───	───	───	───
───	───	───	───
───	───	───	───
───	───	───	───
───	───	───	───
───	───	───	───

Community Gratitude

Growth

- Growth
- Gratitude
- Education
- Vision
- Wisdom

Envision Growth

My Definition:

Scribble

Growth Experience

Positive Power Words

In what areas do I experience growth most frequently?
How can I apply my education positively in my life?
What steps can I take to use this education my life?

Growth

Visual
Support

Growth Affirmation

True Desire	Beginning Date	Ending Date	Outcome
True Desire put into motion has only one option ➡			<u>Completion</u>

———	———	———	———
———	———	———	———
———	———	———	———
———	———	———	———
———	———	———	———
———	———	———	———
———	———	———	———
———	———	———	———
———	———	———	———
———	———	———	———

Growth Gratitude

Envision Gratitude

My Definition:

Scribble

Gratitude Experience

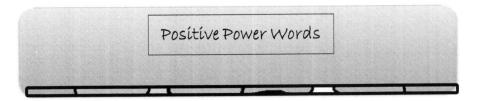

Positive Power Words

What do I have to be grateful for?
How can I express gratitude in my life?
How can I develop daily gratitude in my life?

Gratitude

Visual
Support

Gratitude Affirmation

True Desire	Beginning Date	Ending Date	Outcome
True Desire put into motion has only one option ➡			<u>Completion</u>

Gratitude

Envision Education

My Definition:

Scribble

Education Experience

Positive Power Words

Where have my educational lessons come from?
What are the lessons that I have learned?
How can I apply my knowledge in the future?

Education

Visual
Support

Education Affirmation

True Desire	Beginning Date	Ending Date	Outcome
True Desire put into motion has only one option ➡			<u>Completion</u>

Education Gratitude

Envision Vision

My Definition:

Scribble

Vision Experience

Positive Power Words

What is the vision I have for my life?
Within this vision where am I currently?
How can this vision change my life?

Vision

Visual
Support

Vision Affirmation

True Desire	Beginning Date	Ending Date	Outcome
True Desire put into motion has only one option ➡			<u>Completion</u>
_____	_____	_____	_____
_____	_____	_____	_____
_____	_____	_____	_____
_____	_____	_____	_____
_____	_____	_____	_____
_____	_____	_____	_____
_____	_____	_____	_____
_____	_____	_____	_____
_____	_____	_____	_____
_____	_____	_____	_____

Vision Gratitude

Envision Wisdom

My Definition:

Scribble

Wisdom Experience

What areas in my life have I obtained wisdom?
How can I apply my wisdom positively in my life?
What steps can I take to integrate wisdom in my life?

Wisdom

Visual
Support

Wisdom Affirmation

True Desire	Beginning Date	Ending Date	Outcome
True Desire put into motion has only one option ➡			<u>Completion</u>
▬	▬	▬	▬
▬	▬	▬	▬
▬	▬	▬	▬
▬	▬	▬	▬
▬	▬	▬	▬
▬	▬	▬	▬
▬	▬	▬	▬
▬	▬	▬	▬
▬	▬	▬	▬
▬	▬	▬	▬

Wisdom Gratitude

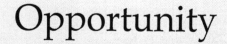

Opportunity

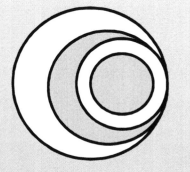

- Opportunity
- Income
- Leisure
- Creativity
- Travel
- Wealth

Envision Opportunity

My Definition:

Scribble

Opportunity Experience

What opportunities do I have in my life?
How have I used these opportunities?
What opportunities do I want in my future?

Opportunity

Visual
Support

Opportunity Affirmation

True Desire	Beginning Date	Ending Date	Outcome
True Desire put into motion has only one option			<u>Completion</u>
———————	———————	———————	———————
———————	———————	———————	———————
———————	———————	———————	———————
———————	———————	———————	———————
———————	———————	———————	———————
———————	———————	———————	———————
———————	———————	———————	———————
———————	———————	———————	———————
———————	———————	———————	———————
———————	———————	———————	———————

Opportunity Gratitude

Envision Income

My Definition:

Scribble

Income Experience

How do I feel when I have income?
How do I see my life with my desired income?
What is my ideal way to create income?

Income

Visual
Support

Income Affirmation

True Desire	Beginning Date	Ending Date	Outcome
True Desire put into motion has only one option ➤			<u>Completion</u>
_____	_____	_____	_____
_____	_____	_____	_____
_____	_____	_____	_____
_____	_____	_____	_____
_____	_____	_____	_____
_____	_____	_____	_____
_____	_____	_____	_____
_____	_____	_____	_____
_____	_____	_____	_____
_____	_____	_____	_____

Income Gratitude

Envision Leisure

My Definition:

Scribble

Leisure Experience

Positive Power Words

How do I spend my leisure time?
How will I incorporate leisure in my daily life?
What do I see myself doing for Leisure in the future?

Leisure

Visual
Support

Leisure Affirmation

True Desire	Beginning Date	Ending Date	Outcome
True Desire put into motion has only one option ➡			Completion

Leisure Gratitude

Envision Creativity

My Definition:

Scribble

Creativity Experience

Positive Power Words

How do I express / use my creativity?
What can I do to increase my creativity?
How can I share my creativity?

Creativity

Visual
Support

Creativity Affirmation

True Desire	Beginning Date	Ending Date	Outcome
True Desire put into motion has only one option ➡			Completion
_____	_____	_____	_____
_____	_____	_____	_____
_____	_____	_____	_____
_____	_____	_____	_____
_____	_____	_____	_____
_____	_____	_____	_____
_____	_____	_____	_____
_____	_____	_____	_____
_____	_____	_____	_____
_____	_____	_____	_____
_____	_____	_____	_____

Creativity Gratitude

Envision Travel

My Definition:

Scribble

Travel Experience

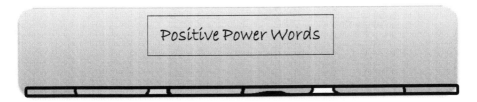

Positive Power Words

Where have I traveled to in my lifetime?
Where do I see myself traveling to in the future?
What experiences will I have during my travels?

Travel

Visual
Support

Travel Affirmation

True Desire	Beginning Date	Ending Date	Outcome
True Desire put into motion has only one option ➡			<u>Completion</u>
————	————	————	————
————	————	————	————
————	————	————	————
————	————	————	————
————	————	————	————
————	————	————	————
————	————	————	————
————	————	————	————
————	————	————	————
————	————	————	————

Travel Gratitude

Envision Wealth

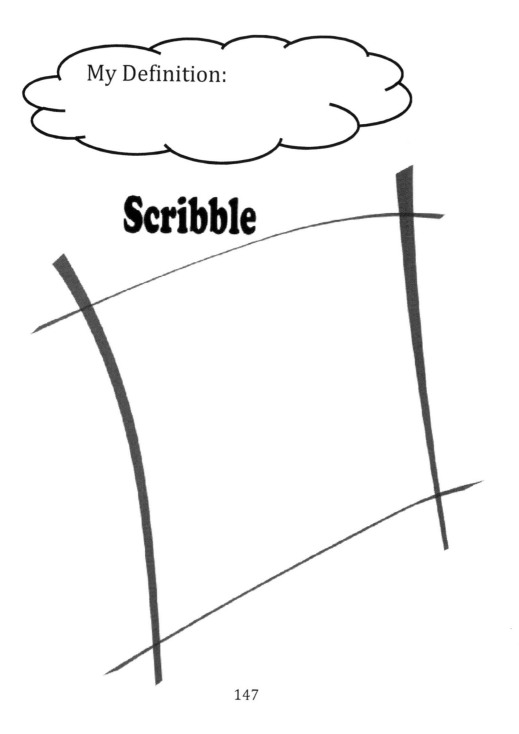

My Definition:

Scribble

Wealth Experience

How does wealth feel to me?
What are my wealth experiences?
How can I help others achieve wealth?

Wealth

Visual
Support

Wealth Affirmation

True Desire	Beginning Date	Ending Date	Outcome
True Desire put into motion has only one option ➡			Completion
————	————	————	————
————	————	————	————
————	————	————	————
————	————	————	————
————	————	————	————
————	————	————	————
————	————	————	————
————	————	————	————
————	————	————	————
————	————	————	————

Wealth Gratitude

Bonus Chapter

Pick my own topics
Fill in the sections

Envision _____

My Definition:

Scribble

_____ Experience

Positive Power Words

_____

_____

_____

Visual Support

_____ Affirmation

True Desire	Beginning Date	Ending Date	Outcome
True Desire put into motion has only one option ➡			Completion

_____	_____	_____	_____
_____	_____	_____	_____
_____	_____	_____	_____
_____	_____	_____	_____
_____	_____	_____	_____
_____	_____	_____	_____
_____	_____	_____	_____
_____	_____	_____	_____
_____	_____	_____	_____
_____	_____	_____	_____

_____ Gratitude

Envision _____

My Definition:

Scribble

_____ Experience

Positive Power Words

_____

_____

_____

Visual
Support

_____ Affirmation

True Desire	Beginning Date	Ending Date	Outcome
True Desire put into motion has only one option ➡			<u>Completion</u>
_____	_____	_____	_____
_____	_____	_____	_____
_____	_____	_____	_____
_____	_____	_____	_____
_____	_____	_____	_____
_____	_____	_____	_____
_____	_____	_____	_____
_____	_____	_____	_____
_____	_____	_____	_____
_____	_____	_____	_____

_____ Gratitude

Envision _____

My Definition:

Scribble

_____ Experience

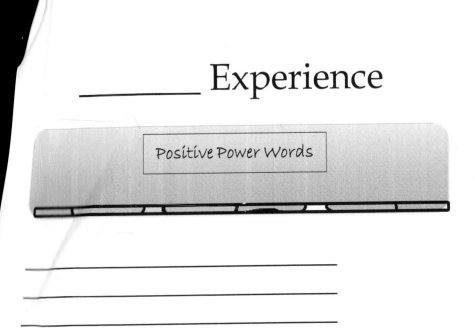

Positive Power Words

Visual
Support

_____ Affirmation

True Desire	Beginning Date	Ending Date	Outcome
True Desire put into motion has only one option ➨			Completion

____	____	____	____
____	____	____	____
____	____	____	____
____	____	____	____
____	____	____	____
____	____	____	____
____	____	____	____
____	____	____	____
____	____	____	____
____	____	____	____

_____ Gratitude

Positive Words

Absolutely
Absorbing
Abundance
Acceptance
Accepted
Accessibility
Accomplishment
Accuracy
Ace
Achieved
Achievement
Acquired
Acted
Active
Activeness
Adaptability
Adjusted
Administered
Admirable
Adoration
Adore
Adventure
Advised
Affection
Affluence
Agility
Agree
Agreeable
Alert
Alertness
Alive
Alluring
Altruism
Amazing
Ambition
Ambitious
Amused
Amusement
Analyzed
Anticipation
Appealing
Applied
Appreciation
Approachability
Approval
Approved
Aroma
Arranged
Articulacy

Assembled
Assertiveness
Assigned
Assurance
Attained
Attentiveness
Attraction
Attractiveness
Audacity
Availability
Award
Awareness
Awe
Balance
Bargain
Beaming
Beats
Beautiful
Beauty
Being
Belonging
Benevolence
Best
Better
Bits
Bliss
Boldness
Boost
Bounce
Boundless
Brave
Bravery
Breakthrough
Breezy
Brief
Bright
Brilliance
Brilliant
Brimming
Budgeted
Built
Buoyancy
Buy
Calculated
Calm
Calmness
Camaraderie
Candor
Capability

Capable
Care
Carefulness
Catalogued
Celebrity
Centralized
Certain
Certainty
Chaired
Challenge
Charity
Charm
Charming
Chastity
Cheerful
Cheerfulness
Chic
Choice
Clarity
Classified
Clean
Cleanliness
Clear
Clear-Mindedness
Cleverness
Closeness
Coached
Colorful
Comfort
Comfortable
Comfy
Commitment
Communicated
Compassion
Compiled
Completed
Completion
Compliment
Composed
Composure
Computed
Conceived
Concentration
Conducted
Confidence
Confident
Congruency
Connection

Positive Words

Connoisseur
Consciousness
Consistency
Consolidated
Constructed
Consulted
Contentment
Continuity
Contracted
Contributed
Contribution
Control
Conviction
Conviviality
Cool
Coolness
Cooperation
Cooperative
Coordinated
Cordiality
Corrected
Correctness
Counseled
Courage
Courageous
Courteous
Courtesy
Coy
Craftiness
Creamy
Created
Creativity
Credibility
Credible
Crisp
Cuddly
Cultured
Cunning
Curiosity
Customized
Daring
Dashing
Dazzling
Debonair
Decisive
Decisiveness
Decorous
Decorum
Decreased
Deference

Defined
Delegated
Delicate
Delicious
Delight
Delightful
Delivered
Deluxe
Demonstrated
Dependability
Dependable
Depth
Designed
Desire
Detailed
Determination
Determined
Developed
Devotion
Devoutness
Dexterity
Diagnosed
Diamond
Difference
Dignity
Diligence
Diligent
Dimple
Directed
Direction
Directness
Discerning
Discipline
Discovery
Discreet
Discretion
Distinctive
Distributed
Diversity
Divine
Dominance
Doubled
Drafted
Dreaming
Dreamy
Drive
Duty
Dynamic
Dynamism
Eager

Eagerness
Easy
Economy
Ecstasy
Ecstatic
Edited
Education
Effectiveness
Effervescent
Efficiency
Efficient
Elated
Elation
Elegance
Eminent
Empathy
Enchanting
Encouraged
Encouragement
Encouraging
Endless
Endurable
Endurance
Energetic
Energy
Enhance
Enhanced
Enjoy
Enjoyment
Enlarged
Enormous
Ensure
Ensured
Entertaining
Entertainment
Enthusiasm
Enthusiastic
Enticing
Essence
Essential
Established
Estimated
Evaluated
Exactly
Examined
Exceeded
Excellence